A Trip to Quebec

Un Voyage
Uhn   Vwah – yahge
à Québec
ah   Kay – bek

BY TERRY SHANNON

PICTURES BY CHARLES PAYZANT

Thanks go to Mr. Normand Gagnon, of the Foreign Language Department, Pasadena (California) City Schools, for his careful work in checking this manuscript.

CHILDRENS PRESS · CHICAGO

allô . . . hello
al-loh (sounds like this in French)

je m'appelle . . . my name is
zhuh ma-pel

Comment vous appelez-vous? . . . What is your name?
kaw-mahn voo-za-play-voo

We are Ann and Peter. We like to travel and meet people and we like to speak other languages. We have taken several exciting trips with our mother and father.

2

Library of Congress Catalog Card Number: 63-15640

Copyright, 1963, Childrens Press.   Printed in the U.S.A.

ma mère . . . my mother   mon père . . . my father
ma mehr   *mohn pehr*

ma soeur . . . my sister   mon frère . . . my brother
ma seuhr   *mohn frehr*

J'aime ma famille. . . . I love my family.
zhaim ma fa-mee-yuh

One day Father said, "We are going to take another trip.
Practice up on your French because that is the language
spoken where we are going."

Où allez-vous? . . . Where are you going?

oo-al-lay-voo

Nous allons à Québec. . . . We are going to Quebec.
noo-za-lohn ah kay-bek

Quelle surprise! . . . What a surprise!
kel suhr-preez

"Good!" we cried. "We're off to France again!" Mother laughed and said, "Guess again. We're not leaving the North American continent." We were puzzled. We looked at a map, then cried, "We know! We're going to Quebec!"

Le Drapeau de Canada   Coat of arms   Le Drapeau de Québec

le drapeau . . . flag
luh drah-poh

Je parle français un peu. . . . I speak French a little.
zhuh parl frahn-seh uhn puh

Parlez-vous anglais? . . . Do you speak English?
par-lay-voo-zahn-gleh

je me souviens . . . I remember
zhuh muh soo-v'yahn

Quebec, which once belonged to France as part of "New France," is the largest province in Canada and Quebec City is its capital. Many French Canadians speak no English, or only a little as a second language.

5

Le fleuve Saint-Laurent

la ville . . . city
la veel

la ville de Québec . . . Quebec City
la veel duh kay-bek

le fleuve Saint-Laurent . . . the Saint Lawrence River
luh fluhve sehn-lau-ranh

Où est l'hôtel? . . . Where is the hotel?
oo eh lo-tel

We drove to Montreal, then went by boat down the St. Lawrence River to Quebec City, the only walled city in North America. From the river we could see the Citadel and the Chateau Frontenac, a hotel that looks like a castle.

Le Château Frontenac

La terrasse Dufferin

numéro de chambre . . . room number
noo-may-roh duh shahm-bruh

la clef . . . the key   la terrasse . . . the terrace
la klay   *la tehr-rahs*

Où est le téléphone? . . . Where is the telephone?
oo eh luh tay-lay-fawn

From our rooms high in the Chateau we could see for miles across the river. Directly beneath us, on top of the bluff, people were strolling on the famous boardwalk, Dufferin Terrace. We walked on the Terrace too.

7

L'ascenseur

un ascenseur . . . an elevator
uhn a-sahn-suhr

en haut . . . up
ahn oh

en bas . . . down
ahn bah

Voulez-vous faire une promenade? . . . Would you like to take a walk?
voo-lay-voo fehr oon prawm-nad

An elevator built on the steep hill joins the two levels
of Quebec City. We rode down in it and walked along the
little cobblestone streets of old lower town.

8

Frère Jacques (Translation on p. 31)

French Folksong

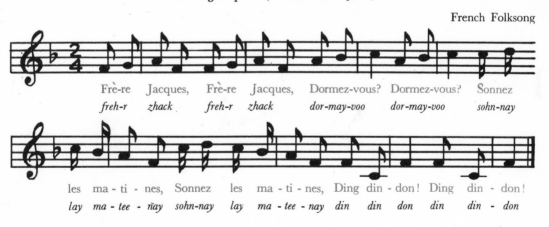

Frè-re Jacques, Frè-re Jacques, Dormez-vous? Dormez-vous? Sonnez
freh-r zhack freh-r zhack dor-may-voo dor-may-voo sohn-nay

les ma-ti-nes, Sonnez les ma-ti-nes, Ding din-don! Ding din-don!
lay ma-tee-nay sohn-nay lay ma-tee-nay din din don din din-don

In the *rue Sous-le Cap (soo-luh cap)*, the narrowest street in North America, children crowded around us. They sang an old French folksong. We knew the song and sang it too.

9

Notre-Dame-des-Victoires

Notre-Dame-des-Victoires . . . Our Lady of Victories
naw-truh-dam-day-vik-twahr

une église . . . a church   le nom . . . the name
oon ay-gleez   *luh nohm*

L'église est très belle . . . The church is very beautiful.
lay-glee-zeh treh bel

We saw a tiny church which was built in 1688 by the French settlers. Grateful for a victory over the British in 1690, the settlers gave the church the name it still bears.

10

Nous montons les escaliers. . . . We climb the stairs.
noo mohn-tohn lays-ehs-ka-lyay

Je suis fatigué. . . . I am tired.   oui . . . yes
zhuh suhee fa-tee-gay   *wee*

Je le regrette. . . . I'm sorry.   non . . . no
zhuh luh ruh-greht

"Up we go!" Father said at the foot of a long flight of steps at the end of a street. We climbed and climbed all the way to the top, which brought us back to upper town.

La Place d'Armes

la calèche . . . carriage
la kal-esh

les chevaux . . . the horses
lay shuh-voh

le cheval brun . . . the brown horse
luh shuh-val bruhn

One day we went for a drive in a *calèche*. Dozens of them wait for passengers in the *Place d'Armes*, the town square. We clip-clopped up through Battlefield Park. Nearly everyone knows it as the Plains of Abraham where an historic battle was fought and France lost Canada to the British.

12

le thé de l'après-midi . . . afternoon tea
luh tay duh la-preh-mee-dee

le thé . . . tea   le café . . . coffee   le chocolat . . . chocolate
luh tay   *luh ka-fay*   *luh shaw-kaw-la*

les sandwichs . . . sandwiches   les gateaux . . . cakes
lay sahn-weesh   *lay gah-toh*

le beurre d'arachide . . . peanut butter
luh buhrr dar-a-sheed

At the Chateau we had afternoon tea in the Champlain
room. Samuel de Champlain was the man who founded
Quebec City in 1608. Musicians in early-day costumes
played during tea.

13

LES ANIMAUX

La mouffette

Le lion

Le singe

L'ours

les animaux . . . the animals
lay-zan-i-moh

un animal . . . an animal
uhn an-i-mahl

le jardin zoologique . . . the zoo
luh zhar-dahn zaw-aw-law-zheek

le lion . . . lion
luh lee-ohn

le singe . . . monkey
luh seenzh

l'ours . . . bear
loor

la mouffette . . . skunk
la moo-feht

We spent a whole day at the zoo. We thought it great fun to hear people speaking in French to the animals. We tried it, too, since the animals didn't understand English.

14

le loup des bois . . . timber wolf (wolf of the woods)
luh loo day bwah

le renard . . . fox
luh reh-nar

le cerf . . . deer
luh sehr

l'otarie . . . sea lion
lo-ta-ree

le castor . . . beaver
luh kas-tor

And we laughed with the French Canadian children at the antics of some of the animals. "Laughter is the same in any language," Mother said.

15

au marché . . . at the market	les fleurs . . . flowers
oh mar-shay	*lay fluhr*
les légumes . . . vegetables	les fruits . . . fruit
lay lay-goom	*lay frwee*
les tomates . . . tomatoes	les petits pois . . . peas
lay taw-mat	*lay puh-tee-pwah*
le chou . . . cabbage	la pomme . . . apple
luh shoo	*la pum*
la pêche . . . peach	la poire . . . pear
la pehsh	*la pwahr*

We went to the outdoor market where farmers bring their produce to sell. Father bought some flowers for Mother.

16

à vendre miel . . . for sale—honey   aujourd'hui . . . today
ah vahn-druh m'yehl   *oh-zhoor-dwee*

le canard . . . duck   le poulet . . . chicken   les oeufs . . . eggs
luh ka-nar   *luh poo-leh*   *lay-zeuh*

Achetons du sucre d'érable . . . Let us buy some maple sugar.
ash-tohn dew soo-kruh day-rah-bluh

Mother bought some little pots of honey. And we bought
some maple sugar. Canadian money is in dollars and cents,
the same as in the United States.

17

L'île d'Orléans . . . The Island of Orleans
leel dor-lay-ahn

la maison . . . the house   la chappelle . . . the chapel
la meh-zohn   *la sha-pel*

le pont . . . bridge   les vaches . . . cows   le cochon . . . pig
luh pohn   *lay vash*   *luh ko-shohn*

One day we went over a bridge to the Island of Orleans. Farm houses there are like those of Normandy and Brittany in France. We saw several little wayside chapels.

18

le moulin à vent . . . windmill
luh moo-lahn ah vahn

le chien . . . dog
luh sh'yehn

les champs . . . the fields
lay shahn

l'arbre . . . tree
lar-bruh

la ferme . . . farm
la fehrmm

le fermier . . . farmer
luh fehr-m'yay

Il fait du vent. . . . The wind is blowing.
eel fay dew vahn

We spoke French with a boy who was plowing the fields.
Then Father took our pictures beside an old windmill.

19

le dîner . . . dinner   chaud . . . warm (hot)   froid . . . cold
luh dee-nay   *shoh*   *frwah*

la soupe . . . soup   la salade . . . salad
la soop   *la sa-lad*

la viande . . . meat   le dessert . . . dessert
la v'yahnd   *luh day-sehr*

L'addition, s'il vous plaît. . . . The check (bill), please.
la-dee-s'yohn seel voo pleh

One warm night we ate in the garden room of a restaurant.
We chose our dinner from the French side of the menu.

20

le jour de fête . . . holiday très gai . . . very gay
luh zhoor duh feht *treh gay*

Saint Jean Baptiste . . . Saint John the Baptist
sehn zhahn ba-teest

J'aime danser et chanter. . . . I like to dance and to sing.
zhaim dahn-say ay shahn-tay

On the eve of an important French Canadian holiday, St. Jean Baptiste Day, there was folkdancing on Dufferin Terrace. St. Jean Baptiste is the patron saint of Quebec. Everyone was very gay and we enjoyed the singing and dancing.

21

les drapeaux . . . flags   un tambour . . . a drum
lay drah-poh   *uhn tam-boor*

rouge . . . red   jaune . . . yellow   bleu . . . blue
roozh   *zhohn*   *bluh*

Nous avons deux ballons. . . . We have two balloons.
noo-za-vohn duh ba-luhn

Regardez le défilé! . . . Look at the parade!
ruh-gar-day luh day-fee-lay

The next day we watched the big parade. The air was full
of excitement. The air was full of balloons, too!

Le Défilé

les hommes . . . men
lay-zum

les garçons . . . boys
lay gar-sohn

vert . . . green
vehr

les jeunes filles . . . girls
lay zhuhn fee-yuh

Tout le monde est heureux. . . . Everyone is happy.
too luh mohnd eh-tuh-ruh

Quoi ensuite? . . . What next?
kwah ahn-suheet

C'est tout! . . . That's all!
seh too

There were colorful floats and pretty girls. There were
marching bands, and men and boys in bright uniforms.

les boutiques . . . shops	la pharmacie . . . drugstore
lay boo-teek	*la far-ma-see*
la librairie . . . bookstore	la bibliothèque . . . library
la lee-breh-ree	*la bee-blyaw-tehk*
un crayon . . . a pencil	un stylo . . . a fountain pen
uhn kreh-yohn	*uhn stee-loh*

Combien est ceci? . . . How much is this?
kawm-be-anh eh suh-see

"This is the day for shopping," Mother said one day. We went to a number of little shops along a quaint street.

à un grand magazin . . . to a department store
ah uhn grahn ma-ga-zehn

par où . . . which way
pa-roo

tout droit . . . straight ahead
too drwah

Je voudrais un collier. . . . I want a necklace.
zhuh voo-dray uhn kaw-l'yay

des gants . . . some gloves
day gahn

une cravate . . . a necktie
oon kra-vat

Then we went to the department stores, which are all on
one street. Father asked a policeman how to get there.

La Porte St. Louis . . . The Saint Louis Gate
la port sehn lew-ee

Il fait beau. . . . It is good weather.
eel feh boh

Allons à la Citadelle. . . . Let's go to the Citadel.
al-lohn ah la see-ta-del

Today, gates in the great wall around Quebec City are unguarded. We went through the St. Louis gate and up the hill to the Citadel. Soldiers still occupy the old fort and we went to see the changing of the guard.

A la Citadelle

les véhicules . . . vehicles
lay vay-hih-kuhl

les piétons . . . pedestrians
lay p'yay-tohn

Voici la sentinelle. . . . Here is the sentinel.
vwah-see la sehn-teh-nel

Le veston du soldat est rouge. The soldier's coat is red.
luh vehs-tohn dew sol-dah eh roozh

The soldiers of the guard belong to a regiment spoken of as "The Queen's Own." They wear uniforms just like those of the soldiers who guard Buckingham Palace in London. But they receive their commands in French.

Voilà beaucoup de soldats. . . . There are many soldiers.
vwah-la boh-koo duh sol-dah

Nous sommes quatre. . . . There are four of us.
noo sum ka-truh

Ecoutez la musique ! . . . Listen to the music !
ay-koo-tay la moo-zeek

The band played while a fresh group of soldiers marched
up to relieve those who had been standing guard.

28

Le bouc est très beau. . . . The goat is very handsome.
luh boo'hk eh treh boh

Merci beaucoup . . . Thank you very much
mehr-see boh-koo

pour le cadeau. . . . for the gift.
poor luh ka-doh

"Look!" we cried. "A goat! He's marching to the music
with the soldiers!" He was Baptiste, the soldiers' mascot,
a gift to the regiment from the Queen of England.

29

Au revoir. . . . Good-by.
oh ruh-vwahr

Bonne chance! . . . Good luck!
bun shahns

The changing of the guard was an exciting ceremony.
When it was over we said good-by to Baptiste and the
soldier in charge of him. Baptiste gave us his version of a
military salute. We laughed. It was amusing to see a goat
down on his knees! We said, "*Au revoir.* We hope to come
back some day." The soldier said, "Good-by. *Bonne chance!*"
It was a wonderful finish to our trip to Quebec.

There are many colorful words sometimes used by French Canadians which are not in the French vocabulary. For the most part they are English words adapted to French through spelling, pronunciation, or both. Here are a few:

French Canadian	English	French
patat	potato	la pomme de terre
patat		*la pum duh tehr*
gazoline	gasoline	l'essence
gaz-oh-leen		*leh-sahns*
les shorts	shorts	le caleçon
lay shorts		*luh kal-sohn*
la machine	car	la voiture
la ma-sheen		*la vwah-tuhr*
le shop	factory	l'usine
luh shop		*lu-zeen*
le grand boss	employer	le patron
luh grahn bos		*luh pa-trohn*
la parade	parade	le défilé
la parahd		*luh day-fee-lay*

French and English sentence structure and literal wording may sometimes differ, but meanings are essentially the same. For example, on page 2, "je m'appelle" is literally "I me call" and "Comment vous appelez-vous?" is "How you call you?" Page 27, "Le veston du soldat est rouge." is literally "The coat of the soldier is red."

Translation of folksong *Frère Jacques* on page 9:
Brother James, Brother James, Are you sleeping? Are you sleeping? Ring the morning bells, Ring the morning bells, Ding ding dong! Ding ding dong!

Days of the week and the names of the months are not capitalized when written in French.

lundi . . . Monday *luhn-dee*	jeudi . . . Thursday *zhuh-dee*
mardi . . . Tuesday *mar-dee*	vendredi . . . Friday *vahn-druh-dee*
mercredi . . . Wednesday *mehr-kruh-dee*	samedi . . . Saturday *sam-dee*

C'est aujourd'hui dimanche. . . . Today is Sunday.
ceh-toh-zhoor-dwee dee-mahnsh

ce matin . . . this morning *suh ma-tehn*	midi . . . noon *mee-dee*
cet après-midi . . . this afternoon *seh-ta-preh-mee-dee*	demain . . . tomorrow *duh-mehn*
janvier . . . January *zhahn-v'yay*	juillet . . . July *zhuee-yeh*
février . . . February *fay-vree-y'ay*	août . . . August *oo*
mars . . . March *marce*	septembre . . . September *sehp-tahm-bruh*
avril . . . April *ah-vreel*	octobre . . . October *awk-taw-bruh*
mai . . . May *meh*	novembre . . . November *naw-vahm-bruh*
juin . . . June *zhuehn*	décembre . . . December *day-sahm-bruh*

le mois d'avril . . . the month of April.
luh mwah da-vreel

DATE DUE

Ap 17			
Dec 22			
3 ap 70			
July 11/70			
Aug 18			
Sept 5			
Sep 19			
CAT. NO. 1137			